ONE WINTER
NIGHT IN AUGUST

X. J. KENNEDY

ONE WINTER NIGHT IN AUGUST

and Other Nonsense Jingles

Illustrated by David McPhail

A MARGARET K. MC ELDERRY BOOK

ATHENEUM   1975   NEW YORK

For Katie, Dave, Matthew,
Dan, and Josh

ACKNOWLEDGMENTS

"Vulture" originally appeared in *Harper's,*
under the title "Ecology." "King Tut" is
from the book *Nude Descending a Staircase,*
copyright © 1961 by X. J. Kennedy. Reprinted
by permission of Doubleday & Company, Inc.

Published simultaneously in Canada by
McClelland & Stewart, Ltd.
Manufactured in the United States of America
Printed by Murray Printing Company
Forge Village, Massachusetts
Bound by H. Wolff, New York
Designed by Suzanne Haldane
First Edition

Library of Congress Cataloging
in Publication Data

Kennedy, X   J
One winter night in August,
and other nonsense jingles.
"A Margaret K. McElderry book."
SUMMARY: More than fifty nonsense rhymes about
a people-eating giant snail, exploding gravy,
a witch, a dragon, and other topics.
[1. Nonsense verses] I. McPhail, David M., ill.
II. Title.   PZ8.3.K384oh   811'.5'4   74-18185
ISBN 0-689-50022-X

CONTENTS

ONE WINTER
NIGHT IN AUGUST

KING TUT

King Tut
Crossed over the Nile
On stepping stones
Of crocodile.

King Tut!
His mother said,
Come here this minute!
You'll get wet feet.
King Tut is dead

And now King Tut
Tight as a nut
Keeps his big fat Mummy shut.

King Tut,
Tut, tut.

MOTHER'S NERVES

My mother said, "If just once more
I hear you slam that old screen door,
I'll tear out my hair! I'll dive in the stove!"
I gave it a bang and in she dove.

STAN STAPLER

My friend Stan Stapler, he's the most!
  I saw his two front teeth
Bite through a stack of buttered toast
  And fold flat underneath.

THE WHALES OFF WALES

With walloping tails, the whales off Wales
Whack waves to wicked whitecaps.
And while they snore on their watery floor,
They wear wet woolen nightcaps.

The whales! the whales! the whales off Wales,
They're always spouting fountains.
And as they glide through the tilting tide,
They move like melting mountains.

EXPLODING GRAVY

My mother's big green gravy boat
Once thought he was a navy boat.

I poured him over my mashed potatoes
And out swam seven swift torpedoes.

Torpedoes whizzed and whirred, and—WHAM!
One bumped smack into my hunk of ham

And blew up with an awful roar,
Flinging my carrots on the floor.

Exploding gravy! That's so silly!
Now all I ever eat is chili.

MINGLED YARNS

What stories are mixed together?

1] Whose cherry tree did young George chop?
It was Pinocchio's.
And every time George told a lie
He grew an inch of nose.

2] Jack be nimble,
Jack be quick,
Jack jump over
The beanstalk stick!

3] Aladdin had a little lamp,
It smelled all keroseny.
And everywhere Aladdin took
His lamp jam-packed with genii.

He tool his lamp to school one day,
Which made the teacher blubber
And all the children laugh to see
Young Al the old lamp-rubber.

THE TROUBLE
WITH A DINOSAUR

The trouble with a dinosaur
Is how to move while ambling
And how to sit and hatch her eggs
Without the whole bunch scrambling.

WICKED
WITCH'S KITCHEN

You're in the mood for freaky food?
You feel your taste buds itchin'
For nice fresh poison ivy greens?
Try Wicked Witch's kitchen!

She has corn on the cobweb, cauldron-hot,
She makes the meanest cider,
But her broomstick cakes and milkweed shakes
Aren't fit to feed a spider.

She likes to brew hot toadstool stew—
"Come eat, my sweet!" she'll cackle—
But if you do, you'll turn into
A jack-o'-lantern's jackal.

COWS

The cows that browse in pastures
Seem not at all surprised
That as they moo they mow the lawn
And their milk comes pasture-ized.

WHO TO PET
AND WHO NOT TO

Go pet a kitten, pet a dog,
Go pet a worm for practice,
But don't go pet a porcupine—

You want to be a cactus?

SNOWFLAKE SOUFFLE

Snowflake soufflé
Snowflake soufflé
Makes a lip-smacking lunch
On an ice-cold day!

You take seven snowflakes,
You break seven eggs,
And you stir it seven times
With your two hind legs.

Bake it in an igloo,
Throw it on a plate,
And slice off a slice
With a rusty ice-skate.

MEDUSA

Medusa's looks had what it takes
    To knock the rust off boilers.
She had a lovely head of snakes,
    She'd put it up in coilers.

She'd give you such a rocky look
    Out of her old eye sockets,
You'd feel your bones all turn to stones
    And pebbles fill your pockets.

MY YELLOW TELEPHONE

I had a yellow telephone,
  Her name was Cally Flower.
Her shoulders shone like precious stone,
  Her purr was packed with power.

At night when I lay tucked in bed,
  She'd ring and slice my slumber
Until I stood her on her head
  And got a secret number.

THE SKELETON WALKS

Right after our Thanksgiving feast
Our turkey's bones went hobblin'
To Joan the wicked witch's house
To be her turkey goblin.

LUCKY SUKEY

Look out, here comes Lucky Sukey
Sucking on her mucky-looking cookie.

She can beat at baseball,
She can run like the wind,
She can chin the bar faster than it's ever been
    chinned.

Look out, here comes Lucky Sukey
Sucking on her mucky-looking cookie.
How can she always win?
                    It's spooky!

ON THE OCEAN FLOOR

A scallop met a polyp
And called out through its shell,
"Say, polyp dear, I have no ear,
I cannot hear too well,
But something's ringing in my head—
Is it a gong, pray tell?"
"Why no, sweet scallop," answered polyp,
"Just a diving bell."

UNUSUAL
SHOELACES

To lace my shoes
I use spaghetti.
Teacher and friends
All think I'm batty.

Let 'em laugh, the whole
Kit and kaboodle.
But I'll get by.
I use my noodle.

SIR PERCIVAL
AND THE DRAGON

"Sir Percival,
Be merciful,"
  The cornered dragon begged.
"There'll never be
Another me
  So mean, so many-legged.

"What fiercer foe
Than I could show
  Your golden-headed charmer
How you don't cringe?—
Who else so singe
  The brightness of your armor?

"Though kings hold sway
And swear they'll pay
  The knight who works my slaughter
Half some dull town,
An old half-crown
  And half their cross-eyed daughter,

"For such reward
Why dent your sword?
  Such deeds seem rash and reckless.
I guard the door
To gold galore—
  Here, have a diamond necklace.

"Tell them at court
They may cavort:
  The dragon they've been dreading
Is now done in.
Display my skin,
  This old one I'm through shedding.

"Your blue eyes flash?
You seek not cash
  But only fame and virtue?
Through dragon lore
Your name shall soar—
  That's not to sneeze at. KER-choo!"

"Quite right, quite right,"
Agreed the knight,
  "I'll give you no more jabs, sir.
Go guard your hoard,
I'll save my sword
  For broiling shish kebabs, sir!"

KANGAROO AND KIWI

A crazy kangaroo I knew
Who'd always giggle ("Tee-hee!")
Grabbed a big flat pie and let it fly
At a little peewee kiwi.

That kiwi, though, she ducked down low
And let that missile miss her.
It circled back and it landed—whack!—
In the kangaroo's own kisser.

Said kiwi, "My, that's tricky pie,
Must be a custard boomerang?"
"No," said kangaroo, smacking her lips,
"It's a lemon kangaroo-meringue."

CONSTRICTOR
RESTRICTER

I feed my boa bowling balls,
Trucks, bikes, and samovars.

Why?
        Well, he may be full of lumps,
But he stays behind his bars.

GIANT SNAIL

My Uncle Artemus McPhail,
Digested by a giant snail,
Has kept on loudly disapproving:
"I find this whole thing hardly moving."

JUGGLER DOUG

While Juggler Doug was juggling jugs,
Along came two potato bugs
   And said, "Say, Doug, you sure can juggle—
   Is juggling jugs much of a struggle?"

"You bet it is, you ugly bugs,"
Said one of Doug the Juggler's jugs.
   "Why, nothing's harder than jug-juggling.
   If I were Doug, I'd switch to smuggling."

Just then, out of that talking jug
There crawled a blinking lightning bug.
   Said he, "When Doug starts in to juggle,
   A jug's a jumpy place to snuggle."

INSTANT STORM

One day in Thrift-Rite Supermart
My jaw dropped wide with wonder,
For there, right next to frozen peas,
Sat frozen French-fried thunder,
Vanilla-flavored lightning bolts,
Fresh-frozen raindrop rattle—
So I bought the stuff and hauled it home
And grabbed my copper kettle.

I'd cook me a mess of homemade storm!
But when it started melting,
The thunder shook my kitchen sink,
The ice-cold rain kept pelting,
Eight lightning bolts bounced round the room
And snapped my pancake turners—
What a blooming shame!
                    Then a rainbow came
And spanned my two front burners.

CENSUS NONSENSE

Said a census taker to a centaur,
"Pardon me, I'm counting.
Sir, are you man or are you horse?
Please, would you mind dismounting?"

SPIDER SNYDER

A man in our town, Caleb Snyder,
Started to become a spider,

Let his whiskers grow a little,
Spun a sticky web of spittle

All the way from the firehouse steeple
To old Miss Mabbott's sugar maple.

Now he's waiting. Patient Snyder!
Ha, what luck! Here comes a glider!

No, I'm wrong—looks like an eagle—
Or—can it be?—an inland sea gull—

Hold on now—she's a helicopter!
He's opened his mouth and in he's popped her!

No, that's not what she is! Oh, hang her,
She's the evening mail plane bound for Bangor!

No, no she isn't! Lucky man,
He's caught the jet bound for Japan!

That's what she is! He's caught the jet
Bound for Japan!
                        (He's not back yet.)

MIXED-UP SCHOOL

We have a crazy mixed-up school.
Our teacher Mrs. Cheetah
Makes us talk backwards. Nicer cat
You wouldn't want to meet a.

To start the day we eat our lunch,
Then do some heavy dome-work.
The boys' and girls' rooms go to us,
The hamster marks our homework.

At recess time we race inside
To put on diving goggles,
Play pin-the-donkey-on-the-tail,
Ball-foot or ap-for-bobbles.

Old Cheetah, with a chunk of chalk,
Writes right across two blackbirds,
And when she says, "Go home!" we walk
The whole way barefoot backwards.

MECHANICAL MENAGERIE

My Uncle Ike's an engineer.
He has the nutty habit
Of building beasts from wheels and wire.
He's built a robot rabbit

That hides in manholes in the street
And lives on tinfoil lettuce.
His brand new chrome-trimmed crocodile
Keeps trying hard to get us.

He has lightning bugs that come with plugs,
Electric eels that boil,
A bat that flies on batteries,
An oyster that you oil,

A forty-four-seat elephant
With a trunk so you can pack her,
And a parrot that says, "Polly want
A lighted cannon cracker!"

FATHER AND MOTHER

My father's name is Frankenstein,
He comes from the Barbados.
He fashioned me from package twine
And instant mashed potatoes.

My mother's name is Draculeen,
She lets a big bat bite her,
And folks who sleep here overnight
Wake up a few quarts lighter.

NAILS

My father says he's hard as nails,
   But, hanging pictures, often
He hammers on his fingernails.
   Oh, how that makes him soften!

GREAT-GREAT GRANDMA, DON'T SLEEP
IN YOUR TREEHOUSE TONIGHT

Great-great Grandma, don't sleep in your tree-
  house tonight,
    Don't swing on your rope and your tire,
'Cause your tree felt the bite
Of a mighty termite—
      Have a seat
      By the heat
Of the fire!

Here's a big bowl of black bolts and nuts you can
  crack,
    Here's some cider to slide down your craw,
      Oh, what fun it'll be
      While we roast that old tree—
        None so tall
        Stands in all
Arkansas!

AT THE POOL

Crawling to the edge to drool,
Robert tumbled in the pool.

The lifeguard gave a whistle-blast—
"Help! I can't swim! He's filling fast!"

The oldest lady still alive
Saved Robert with a jackknife dive.

And when we turned him upside down
He poured so long I thought I'd drown.

HELP!

Firemen, firemen!
State police!
Victor's locked in Pop's valise!
Robert's eating kitty litter!
Doctor!
          Lawyer!
                    Baby-sitter!

A SOCIAL MIXER

Father said, "Heh, heh! I'll fix her!"—
Threw Mother in the concrete mixer.

She whirled about and called, "Come hither!"
It looked like fun. He jumped in with her.

Then in to join that dizzy dance
Jumped Auntie Bea and Uncle Anse.

In leaped my little sister Lena
And Chuckling Chuck, her pet hyena.

Even Granmaw Fanshaw felt a yearning
To do some high-speed overturning.

All shouted through the motor's whine,
"Aw come on in—the concrete's fine!"

I jumped in too and got all scrambly.
What a crazy mixed-up family!

CLEANING HOUSE

Our baby eats our rugs so clean
He beats a carpet sweeper.
We'd change our vacuum-cleaner bag,
But changing baby's cheaper.

SPECIAL DELIVERY

The mailman brought our dog back home
And told us not to let him out.
It seems he tried to ride about
The nation with a ten-cent stamp
Stuck to his forehead, but the rate
Is more than that for one his weight.

WAKING UP UNCLE

My uncle, General Doug MacDougal,
Sleeps nights inside a huge blue bugle.
And when I'm feeling mean and devilly,
I blow him a bit of red-hot reveille.

He naps each noon. My favorite gag
Is filling Uncle's sleeping bag
With prune whip yogurt to the brim.
It certainly surprises him
To jump in whistling happy tunes,
Then ooze back out, all gooey prunes.

He always chases me nine miles
And grabs me by the neck and smiles
And says, "You've goofed again, you loafer—
Vanilla! *That*'s the kind I go for!"

BOBBY BOASTER
AND HIS TOASTER

Bobby Boaster
Took his toaster
Riding on a roller coaster.

They clicked to the peak of the highest hill.
"Oh!" cried the toaster, "we're starting to spill!"

Said Bobby, "Aw, you crumby coward!
Too bad this car's not rocket-powered!"

They roared like thunder round a rail.
The toaster's toast looked deathly pale.

They clanked uphill, then down they coasted.
"Hey, look, I'm standing!" Bobby boasted.

All of a sudden the coaster stopped.
Both the toast and Bobby popped.

He boasted all the way to Jupiter,
"I'm the stupidest boy! Nobody's stupider!"

MY BIRTHDAY CAKE

My birthday cake's so full of eggs
It cackles, clucks, and scratches,
And every time it ups and lays,
A cupcake with a candle on it hatches.

A MONSTROUS MOUSE

Just as I'd sucked in wind to take
A giant puff at my birthday cake,

While all the children sang and cheered,
Up shot the window shade—in peered

A monstrous mouse with jagged jaws!
Into the kitchen poked two paws

With fingernails like reindeer antlers!
The way a team of house-dismantlers

Bash houses down with a swinging ball,
He kicked—boom!—no more kitchen wall—

And through a new door to our kitchen
That wicked mouse, his whiskers twitchin',

Grabbed hold of my cake plate by both handles
And shouted, "Yum! what nice hot candles!"

Straight through my cake his head went—squish!
I didn't have time to make a wish.

But when he pulled himself back out,
All fresh fruit frosting, his whole snout

Was fire! Sparks sputtered from each whisker!
You never did see mouse-dancing brisker.

Thick clouds of smoke choked our apartment.
My father phoned the Fire Department.

Up screeched four fire trucks, sirens roaring—
Nobody found *my* party boring!

Our bowl of orangeade and ice
Proved just the thing for dunking mice.

Mouse ran outside and down his tunnel
Faster than water through a funnel.

I sort of forget what games we played.
Nobody drank much orangeade.

THE CABOOSE WHO
WOULDN'T COME LAST

I know a little red caboose
  Who one day grew so weary
Of coming last, it broke off loose
  And rolled right to a dairy.

"Just what I need!" the milkman cried,
  "A red caboose who differs!"—
And now it leads a whole parade
  Of cows and calves and heifers.

A COUGHDROP LIES
IN MY DOGHOUSE

A coughdrop lies in my doghouse
Gnawing an old cow shin.

I creep up close on hands and knees
To ask, "Where did my dog go, please?"

Says he, "Forgive my being rude,
But I'd rather chew, kid, than be chewed."

AN ALARMING SANDWICH

While munching my salami sub
I heard a small voice call, "Hey, bub,
Ahoy, ahoy! Are you the dope
Put mustard on my periscope?"

SEA HORSE
AND SAWHORSE

A sea horse saw a sawhorse
On a seesaw meant for two.
"See here, sawhorse," said sea horse,
"May I seesaw with you?"

"I'll see, sea horse," said sawhorse.
"Right now I'm having fun
Seeing if I'll be seasick
On a seesaw meant for one."

PLANETS

At night when planets light the sky,
  I bathe and leave a pattern
Of three rings round my tub. That's why
  They call me Soily Saturn.

CATERPILLAR ON A PILLAR

On a cold sand dune in the desert
Stands a pillar alone and tall.
Along comes a fat caterpillar
And up she begins to crawl

Up, up to the top of the pillar
Where she perches and stares all around
Out over the lonely sand dunes
Where the wind is the only sound,

And then that fat caterpillar
Starts in to caterwaul:
"Oh, it's lofty on top of a pillar,
But it won't be much fun if I fall."

Then down from the clouds to the pillar
A stork of the desert glides
And she gulps up that fat caterpillar
And she gulps up that pillar besides.

VULTURE

The vulture's very like a sack
   Set down and left there drooping.
His crooked neck and creaky back
   Look badly bent from stooping
Down to the ground to eat dead cows
   So they won't go to waste
Thus making up in usefulness
   For what he lacks in taste.

GUMBALLS

My gumballs come from a machine,
But when it's out of any,
I pop my penny in my mouth
And blow a giant penny.

A NERVOUS SEA CAPTAIN
FROM CHEESEQUAKE

A nervous sea captain from Cheesequake
Delighted in earthquake and seasquake.
  Said he, " 'Tisn't the noise
  That I truly enjoys,
But those xylophone notes when my knees quake."

ONE WINTER
NIGHT IN AUGUST

How many things are
wrong with this story?

One winter night in August
While the larks sang in their eggs,
A barefoot boy with shoes on
Stood kneeling on his legs.

At ninety miles an hour
He slowly strolled to town
And parked atop a tower
That had just fallen down.

He asked a kind old policeman
Who bit small boys in half,
"Officer, have you seen my pet
Invisible giraffe?"

"Why, sure, I haven't seen him."
The cop smiled with a sneer.
"He was just here tomorrow
And he rushed right back next year.

"Now, boy, come be arrested
For stealing frozen steam!"
And whipping out his pistol,
He carved some hot ice cream.

54

Just then a pack of dogfish
Who roam the desert snows
Arrived by unicycle
And shook the policeman's toes.

They cried, "Congratulations,
Old dear! Surprise, surprise!
You raced the worst, so you came in first
And you didn't win any prize!"

Then turning to the boyfoot bear,
They yelled, "He's overheard
What we didn't say to the officer!
(We never said one word!)

"Too bad, boy, we must turn you
Into a loathsome toad!
Now shut your ears and listen,
We're going to explode!"

But then, with an awful holler
That didn't make a peep,
Our ancient boy (age seven)
Woke up and went to sleep.

MOTHER,
A DOG IS AT THE DOOR

Mother, a dog is at the door
Demanding your moleskin hat.
  No, daughter my child, it drives dogs wild,
  We don't dare give him that.

Mother, he said he'd take instead
Your billy goat's old canoe.
  Good gracious, no! That isn't to go,
  It's stuck fast with airplane glue.

Mother, he'd trade some lemonade
For your bicycle-pumpkin pie.
  Oh, would he, the bum? If I lost one crumb
  Of that delicate stuff I'd die!

Mother, I'm scared! He's all bristly-haired!
He's foaming like canned whipped-cream!
  Tell him, my dear, that indeed I fear
  I shall stand on my head and scream.

Oh, Mother, he's peeling his teeth away—
It's Father in dog's disguise!
  Why, daughter my own, I ought to have known
  That a dog wouldn't want my pies.

COCOA SKIN COAT

If I had a coat
Made of cocoa skin

With marshmallow buttons
Up to my chin,

I'd skip on my toes,
I'd skim on my tummy

In my cocoa skin coat
All warm and scummy!